How to Write the Perfect Sales Page

(Even If You're Not a Copywriter)

The 12-Step Sales Page Template

By: Nathan Fraser

Edited By: Shannon Moore

Copyright © 2019 Nathan Fraser LLC

All rights reserved.

ISBN-13: 978-1-7958-4034-7

DEDICATION

For Isabella.

You are my reason why.

Everything I do, I do for you, so you might have more opportunities than I did.

Whatever you choose to do in life, knowing how to sell will make you more successful at it.

Take this knowledge and apply it to your dreams.

May they all come true.

I love you.

CONTENTS

	Acknowledgments	i
	Forward	ii
1	From High School Drop-Out to High Paid Copywriter	1
2	It Doesn't Matter What You Sell If You Don't Know How to Sell It	4
3	Welcome to the World of Direct Response Copywriting	33
4	The Perfect Sales Page	33
5	Section 1 - The Headline	33
6	Section 2 - The Hook	33
7	Section 3 - Unique Selling Proposition	33
8	Section 4 - Features and Benefits	33
9	Section 5 - Make Your Offer / Call to Action	33
10	Section 6 - Bullets	33
11	Section 7 – Testimonials	33
12	Section 8 - Frequently Asked Questions	33
13	Section 9 - Your Second Call to Action	33
14	Section 10 - Adding Scarcity	33
15	Section 11 - Risk Reversal	33
16	Section 12 - PostScript Selling	33
17	Section 12.5 – Last Call	33

ACKNOWLEDGMENTS

"If I have seen further it is by standing on the shoulders of Giants." -Isaac Newton

There are too many people to thank.

Much of what I've learned came from books written before I was even born.

Eugene Schwartz, Dan Kennedy, Claude Hopkins, and Gary Halbert all had a huge impact on the way I write my sales pages.

Copywriters like Joe Schriefer, Ben Settle, and David Garfinkel have all influenced my style by being there as personal mentors for me.

For them, I am forever grateful.

Lastly, a great big "Thank You" to Shannon Moore, my editor. Without him, many sections of this book would have looked like a garbled mess of word salad.

FORWARD

For a guy who hates school, Nathan Fraser sure is dedicated to education.

I know that's a snarky thing to say. But I can say it confidently and without apology.

Why?

Because Nathan's a man after my own heart. As you will see in the next few pages, he figured out early that school didn't stand a chance of teaching him what he needed to learn. I'm the same way. Except—I took a lot longer before I threw up my hands and said, "Forget about it. If I want to get educated, I need to seek out people who want to teach what I need to learn."

Listen. If you want to learn how to make money in your own business, Nathan can teach you what you need to learn about attracting prospects and turning them into customers, using the written word. This book is an excellent way to start learning from Nathan.

Or, if you've been studying copywriting for a while and you are confused and frustrated by all of the bluster and bravado of the gurus who insist on making it complicated and mystical, what Nathan has to say is like a breath of fresh air. He makes it simple and easy to understand.

I can say that confidently, too, because I know my way around the copywriting world. Copywriting is such a valuable skill with such great money-making potential that it's just bound to attract all kinds of people. Some with good intentions but terrible teaching skills. Some who could charm the skin off a snake, but don't give a rat's ass whether you actually learn anything that will do you any good.

Then there are the men and women I call "the good guys."

They are few in number but worth seeking out and keeping track of. Lucky for you, you've found one already in the author of this book. Nathan truly cares, and he's worked hard to refine his knowledge and skills so he can put his caring to good use. For you. As a (now or future) copywriter and entrepreneur.

How I know this:

Nathan and I met online, and one day he offered to produce a podcast for me. I'd been wanting to do a show for a while, but I hadn't found the right person yet. Nathan was, and is, the right person. He knows what makes a podcast work. He's an excellent producer. He's insatiably curious, in just the right way. Which makes him so dedicated to education (as I mentioned earlier).

Good educators understand what they do is a two-way street. One side of the street, of course, is teaching others. But the other side of the street is continuing to learn themselves. And that describes Nathan, certainly in the copywriting and marketing space.

As I write this, Nathan and I have just completed our 100th podcast. Working with him is fun, and it's worthwhile for me in a number of ways. Of course, along the way I've gotten to know Nathan pretty well. It's a good working relationship, and a good friendship, too.

Being a gifted teacher is great, but for entrepreneurs and professional copywriters, a gifted teacher is not enough. You need a gifted teacher who has been there and done that. Even better, you want someone who's active today in the ways of getting products and services to customers who want and need those products or services.

Now, nobody wants peace more than the seasoned warrior. But make no mistake, doing business is a war. You have a lot of obstacles and a lot of incoming threats. You have to be able to deal with all of them as you grow a business and continue to make customers happy.

Nathan knows all this. He's started and run businesses, and he's very much active in the world of business today, even as you read this. He's made people a lot of money and he knows how to teach what he does. That makes this book especially worth your time.

I hope you'll get the opportunity to know Nathan, as I have. Doing so really will change your life for the better. And reading this book is a very good first step.

-David Garfinkel
Author, Breakthrough Copywriting

NATHAN FRASER

FROM HIGH SCHOOL DROP-OUT TO HIGH PAID COPYWRITER

My third week into kindergarten, the school called my mom to see if I was okay.

Confused, she replied the only way she could. "Yeah, is there something I should be concerned about?"

"Well," the voice on the phone went on, "he hasn't been here all week and we haven't heard from you. We thought maybe he was ill. We were worried it was bad enough that you'd forgotten to call and let us know."

Of course, I wasn't ill. I'd just decided I didn't like school, so I stopped going.

When I got home that day, my mom was worried sick. "Where have you been all day?" she shouted.

"School," I lied, but she saw right through it. I knew right away I was in big trouble.

After a few hours alone in my room, I decided to come clean. I told her I didn't like school and I didn't want to go anymore. I told her the teacher was mean, the kids picked on me, and so, instead of walking to school each day, I went the local park and played until I saw the other kids walking home.

From that day on, a truant officer came each morning to pick me up and drive me to school. I was off to a great start in life.

For the next few days, I'd wait until first recess, then sneak off to the park and continue my normal routine. This went on for about a week before the principal decided I just wasn't ready for school yet. They thought it'd be best if I waited a year and tried again when I was six.

Less than a month in and I was already a drop-out. This was the first thing to go on my "permanent record."

The fact is, I've never done well with authority. I've failed out of more classes than I can remember. I've been arrested quite a few times and always fought my court cases pro se. I've had my ass kicked more than once for standing up to bullies and I never did well in corporate America.

As far back as I can remember, I'd always wanted to be a business owner; to be my own boss. Letting other people boss me around never sat well with me. So, when I was 19, my brother and I started our own record label. When I was 23, I started my own t-shirt company. When I was 29, I launched a graffiti-based cake decorating software.

Like most entrepreneurs with big dreams and little cash flow, I drove those businesses into the ground. Each one, a bigger failure than the last.

The last one, a software company, cost my team two years of hard work, thousands of wasted dollars, and blew up in our faces. Our main investor tried holding us hostage at the distribution level. We found ourselves with a finished product and no way to sell it.

I'd bought into the myth about building a better mousetrap, but nobody was beating a path to our door. We had something great to sell, but no idea how to sell it. Another failure in a long line of disappointments.

By the time I'd started my fourth business, Podcast Blastoff, I knew we needed to do something different. If this one didn't work, I was giving up for good. This was it. All the chips were on the table. It was time for me to man up or shut up.

I crawled back to my team, tail tucked between my legs, and presented my new idea. But why should they trust me after the last time I struck out at bat? They had no reason. So, with my most convincing voice, I explained why this time would be different.

"I've been studying marketing," I told them. "I'm learning how to write sales copy."

"You guys do great work," I continued. "Our problem has always been that I've never figured out how to sell what you produce. Well, that's ending today. If you give me one more chance, I promise to learn everything I can about marketing and how to write ads. I will learn how to sell."

That decision changed the course of our business and the rest of my life. Our next project was the first one to become profitable. It went on to bring in recurring revenue, month after month. I wrote sales pages, emails, and Facebook posts to attract new customers. That was in 2013, and Podcast Blastoff is still going strong to this day.

Beyond the success of Podcast Blastoff, learning about marketing opened up a world of opportunities for me. Since then, I've been blessed to work on projects with some of the biggest names in the marketing industry. From Landon Porter to David Garfinkel, from Ben Settle to Joe Schriefer of Agora Financial, I've been lifted up by some of the greats.

I've made a lot of money for myself and for my clients. I've written for a ton of different niches; from software and video games to dog training and biz ops, from real estate to the fitness industry and more. And it all comes back to the decision I made when I hit rock bottom; the decision to learn the art of sales copy.

Figuring out how to write sales pages changed my life. It took me from being an underemployed High School drop-out to working with some of the most successful people in the world. It took me from being a failed business owner to having a steady flow of income, month after month. Learning how to write successful sales pages changed my life for the better… and now I want to pass that knowledge on to you.

IT DOESN'T MATTER WHAT YOU SELL IF YOU DON'T KNOW HOW TO SELL IT

You've been lied to.

Somewhere along the line, someone told you it's the best products that rise to the top. They told you "if you build a better mousetrap, the world will beat a path to your door." But they forgot to tell you the most important part of that sentence, which is "IF THEY KNOW ABOUT IT."

You see, it's not always the best product that wins in a free market. It's often the best-advertised product that wins. And here's the dirty little secret of the marketing community; not all advertising is created equal. Just because something works for the big brand-named businesses doesn't mean it'll work for yours.

When most people think of advertising, they think repetition, repetition, repetition. Words like "Brand Awareness" come to mind. They remember clever commercials aired on the Super Bowl. Maybe they envision an annoying car salesman in a cheap business suit.

Yes, those are all forms of advertising, but that's not what this book is about. Those ads are what we call Brand Advertising. They work great if you have a war chest for your ad budget. But they're a waste of money for most business owners out there.

For Nike and McDonald's, keeping your name in the public eye might be worth the cost of wasted ad space. Notice I said "might". A lot of research indicates that brand awareness doesn't actually influence our buying decisions like we think it does. And here's the worst part: if you ask most people what was being advertised in one of these catchy commercials, they often have no idea.

Forget about jingles. Forget about fuzzy bears and talking

frogs. Forget about paying for 27 impressions before someone finally decides to take an action. Throw everything you think you know about advertising out the window. What I'm about to show you is something different, altogether.

WELCOME TO THE WORLD OF DIRECT RESPONSE COPYWRITING

Learning about direct response sales copy turned my business around. To this day, it's still the backbone of my marketing. It works for all kinds of advertising in a ton of different media. What we cover here is how to apply the principles of direct response copywriting on your website's sales page.

Direct response copywriting isn't about winning awards or coming up with catchy jingles. It's about getting a response. It's about getting sales. It's about taking the reader on a journey, painting the picture of a better world, and delivering them to a "Buy Now" button at the end.

What you're about to discover is the formula I've used to pull in tens of thousands of dollars for myself and hundreds of thousands of dollars for my clients. It's worked in every industry I've written for and it's based on advice I've received from some of the top copywriters in the world.

Put simply, it works.

It's a rock-solid template for writing sales pages and if you're selling something online, it'll work for you. Use this formula for your sales page and you'll get more conversions than you would have, otherwise.

What follows is a step-by-step walkthrough. We'll cover everything from your headline to your sales pitch, in detail. By the end of this book, you'll have the winning formula your competition only dreams about. You'll have the perfect recipe for a high-converting sales page, and you won't have to pay someone like me thousands of dollars to write it for you.

Are you ready?

THE PERFECT SALES PAGE

What I'm about to show you can be used for all kinds of sales messages. You could use this formula to draft your emails. You could use it to write your sales letters. It's a time-tested template that worked long before the invention of online stores.

The template you're about to discover is based upon the fundamentals of direct response copywriting. However, I've tailored it specifically for online sales pages to get you more sales from your website visitors.

A large portion of my clients hire me to write or fix their sales pages for them. Since more and more sales are happening on the internet these days, having a killer sales page is a necessity. So, if you have a website and something to sell, this is the book for you.

This template will cover the twelve sections I include on almost every sales page I write. For each section, I'll explain what needs to happen, how to make it happen, and I'll include the best examples I can to further illustrate my points.

You're going to get the basic elements every sales page should include and the order they should appear in. That way, your sales page will have the perfect flow to keep people reading all the way to the end. After all, if they don't keep reading, they'll never reach the "Buy Now" button, and that's the whole point of having a sales page in the first place.

So, without any further ado, let's jump into it.

What We'll Cover

First of all, let's take a quick look at what we'll be covering.

These 12 sections will make up the outline of your sales page. I'll go through and explain each one in detail, how to write them, what to include, and what their job is. This is an important point to understand; each section has a job.

The point of this formula is to simulate a sales conversation you might have with your reader. That conversation would have a natural flow and you'd have to cover certain points if you wanted to get to the sale. A sales page works the same way. It needs to hit certain points, in a certain order.

Before we get started, get familiar with each piece of this formula, as part of the greater whole. Your sales page should include each section, in the order they appear here.

- Headline
- Hook
- Unique Selling Proposition
- Features and Benefits
- An Offer / Call to Action
- Bullets
- Testimonials
- FAQ's
- 2nd Call to Action
- Elements of Scarcity
- Risk Reversal
- PostScript Selling / 3rd Call to Action

Now, let's jump in and cover each section, one at a time.

SECTION 1 - THE HEADLINE

How to Write a Killer Headline
(Even if You're Not a Copywriter)

Think about your average day.

You wake up, stretch and yawn. Before you're even out of bed, there are a million things vying for your attention. You roll over, shut off the alarm on your phone... and you're met with 18 notifications.

Facebook messages, emails waiting for you, new videos from your favorite YouTubers. Where to even begin? You turn on the TV to catch the latest propaganda and check on how your stocks are doing. Then, it's off to work you go.

Newspapers, magazines, billboards, TV shows, movies; all part of your daily routine. You're on sensory overload. And guess what... so are the people you're advertising to.

Your ad has to cut through all that noise, get them to stop what they're doing, and make them pay attention to you.

You'd better have a damn good headline.

Your headline is the ad for your ad. Its job is to sell your visitors on why they should keep reading. If the headline doesn't get them invested, they won't even see the rest of your sales page.

Some copywriters claim that the headline counts for up to 80% of the effectiveness of your sales page. I don't know if I'd go that far, but it's definitely important. This is your chance to make a first impression with your visitor. You don't want to screw it up.

Great Headlines Make a Bold Promise

Imagine you only had five seconds to promise your prospect one thing. You're at their front door, trying to make an offer, and they've given you one sentence to get their interest. You can only promise them one thing to get and keep their attention... what would that promise be? That promise should be included in your headline.

Do this in a way that evokes curiosity in your reader.

You don't want to give everything away in the first line; just enough to pique their interest and make them want more. Tell them what you have for them, but let them know they need to keep reading to find out how to get it.

Your headline should also make it clear that what you have is specifically for them.

When they land on your sales pages, they need to know they're in the right place. Otherwise, they'll bounce back to whatever search result brought them there in the first place. Don't be afraid to exclude anyone who isn't the exact person you're trying to sell to. If you try to sell to everybody at once, you'll end up selling to nobody.

Think of it like this;

You're in a crowded room with 1,000 other people. There's loud music playing in the background. Everybody's talking to each other and having a good time, including you. You see a guy wearing a red hat and a green shirt. In the middle of all the commotion, someone just picked his pocket.

Your headline needs to speak directly to him and let him know exactly why he should listen to you. "Hey everyone, that guy just took somebody's wallet" isn't gonna do it.

Instead, you need to say something like "Hey you, in the red hat. Yeah, you. That guy right there stole your wallet and he's making a run for the exit. You'd better stop him."

See how that would work better for getting someone's attention in a crowd? Your headline needs to do that. The internet is a crowded place and if your headline doesn't speak directly to your reader, and only to your reader, they're not going to pay any attention to you.

To speak directly to your reader, you need to know what they're already thinking. You need to "Join the conversation that's already going on in your prospect's mind," as Robert Collier was famous for saying. If you can speak to their greatest desires or their darkest fears in your headline, they're going to keep reading.

I like speaking to both their desires and their fears with my headlines. A great way to do this is with the "Get This, Without That" headline formula. Basically, you promise to get them their desired result without the unwanted side effect they usually associate with it. Of course, you must be able to make good on this promise, but that should go without saying.

Here's an example of the "Get This, Without That" headline;

"How to Start a Business for Under $100"

If you're in the biz-op niche, your market is looking for an easy way to start a business. The problem is, most businesses require lots of cash up-front to get started. When people hear you talking about a new opportunity, the first thing they think is; "How much this is gonna cost me?" How to Start a Business for Under $100 speaks to their desire (staring a business), while alleviating their biggest related concern (start-up cost) at the same time.

Another example of this headline is as follows:

"Who Else Wants a Beach Body This Summer Without Having to Slave Away in the Gym?"

If your market is looking to slim up in time for summer, long strenuous workouts are probably something they're dreading. Some people live for the gym. Those people don't need your solution.

Everybody else who wants what you have to offer likely fears the hard work which accompanies it. If you can promise them the body they want, without the workouts they dread, they're reading the rest of your sales page. It's that simple.

So, what's the best promise you could make about what you sell? What's the one thing your reader really wants to hear? Take that and make it the first part of your headline.

Now, what's the biggest objection they have to that promise? What's one thing they hate that always stands in the way of them getting their desired outcome? Does your solution help them get their desired outcome without having to suffer through the thing they want to avoid? If so, add that in as the second part of your headline and you've got a guaranteed winner.

"Get This Desired Result Without That Unwanted Side Effect" is a great way to grab your reader's attention, make them a promise, and evoke their curiosity, all in one fell swoop.

SECTION 2 - THE HOOK
How to "Hook" Your Readers In

So, you've got your reader's attention... now what?

Well, now you've got to get them invested.

The job of your headline is to get them to read your hook. The goal for your hook is to get them to read the rest of your sales page. Here's where you want to pull them in and give them a reason to keep reading. There are lots of different ways to do this. Let me show you two of my favorites.

Story Driven Hooks

First of all, I love using stories for hooks. They work great as a hook for a few reasons.

When people hear a sales pitch, their defenses go up. When they hear a story, they let their guard down. They let you take control of their thinking. Plus, stories help your reader discover the solution on their own. When we come to our own conclusion about something through a story, we feel like we own that idea; we embrace that idea.

As humans, we have a primal instinct that drives us to listen to stories. Ever since we lived in tribes and sat around campfires, we've been captivated by stories. It's how the elders passed on knowledge from one generation to the next. It's how we learned life lessons, without being subject to the danger of a situation. Listening to stories is a survival instinct. So, if you want visitors to read your sales page, starting with a story can make it happen.

There are a couple tricks to making a story work. Your reader should be able to see themselves in the hero. The hero should be striving for an end goal that your visitor can relate with. Something should be standing in their way. And lastly, whatever you sell should be what helps them reach that end goal.

What that end goal is can vary, depending on what you sell.

If you sell a luxury cruise, the end goal could be a romantic week away or the experience of a lifetime. If you sell a nutritional supplement, the end goal might be better health, more time with the grandkids, or a better sex life. If you sell an online course, the end goal might be more money or a higher social status. What does your reader really want from you? Create a story of transformation that ties in with that.

You can tell them about how you discovered the solution, created the solution, or enjoyed the results of the solution. You can tell a story about the results a real-life client or customer had after using your solution. You can tell a story about a fictional character in the same spot your reader finds themselves, and how your solution improved their imaginary life; just be clear that it's a fictional story.

Remember, whatever story you use, make sure it includes the above-mentioned elements; 1) A relatable hero, 2) A worthy goal, and 3) An obstacle your offer helps them overcome.

Benefit Driven Hooks

My other favorite way to hook a reader in is by jumping straight to the benefits. Benefit driven hooks get straight to why they're here in the first place. There's no beating around the bush. We're getting straight to the point.

What result do they want that you can give them? Lead with that. Oh, and make sure you're talking directly to your reader when you do this.

If you're selling a business opportunity, a benefit-driven hook might look like this:

"Would you like to earn more money in your free time than most people do all month in their full-time jobs? What if you could get started with no investment or experience needed? How great would it be if you could quit your job, today?"

No story. Instead, we get straight to the benefits. But you can see how that would pique the interests of your website visitor. Let's take a look at another example.

Let's say you sell basketball shoes, a great benefit-driven hook might look like this;

"Imagine adding 6 inches to your vertical. How would that improve your game? Let our new basketball shoes turn you into the MVP you're meant to be."

Starting to get the point? Good, now let's talk about when you should use each style of hook and why.

Story driven hooks should be used on colder audiences. If the person visiting your sales page has never heard of you, they're not gonna believe your claims before they get to know you. The less aware your reader is with you or your offer, the better it is to start your hook with a story. So, if you're an off-brand basketball shoe, you'll want to start with a story. If you're Nike, on the other hand, it makes sense to jump straight to the benefits.

So, what kind of traffic is viewing your sales page? Are they coming from Google search, a Google ad or a Facebook ad? Did you target them based on demographics or through a re-pixeling campaign? Are they coming from an email or webinar, or did they find your sales page through a referral link?

The type of traffic you're driving should determine the type of hook you use on your sales page.

SECTION 3 - UNIQUE SELLING PROPOSITION

Why Should I Buy from You?

There's no such thing as a "first to market" advantage. In fact, the surest way to fail as an entrepreneur is to dream up some revolutionary new solution that nobody's asking for.

Sure, you might have a great idea, but educating people on why they need it is almost always more trouble than it's worth. If nobody else is selling it yet, there's a good reason why. It's because there isn't a market for it.

Now, if you're a giant corporation with a war chest for R&D, you can afford to waste money on new ideas and having them fail. But if you're a small or medium-sized business owner like me, it's best to avoid being a pioneer. After all, "pioneers return with a back full of arrows," if they return at all.

So, If I'm gonna sell something, it's gotta be something people are already buying, but with a twist. This way, I don't have to convince them on why they need to buy it. I just need to convince them on why they should buy it from me, rather than from the other guy. That's where having a USP (Unique Selling Proposition) comes into play.

Up until now, your sales page has been about getting your visitor invested in reading more. You spoke to their needs and desires. They feel connected and know you understand them. Now's the best time to tell them about how you can help them. To do that, you'll have to talk about yourself, but in a way that doesn't have them tuning out completely.

So, What's Your Unique Selling Proposition?

What sets your offer apart from other offers on the market? Is it a difference your reader will care about? Your USP needs to make you desirably different. It needs to answer the question; "why should we buy from you, rather than from your competition?"

Let's take a look at a few different types of USPs, shall we?

The Personal Brand USP

The truth is, you might be your own USP.

You might be what makes your offer more desirable than the next one. Your experience or personality might be what makes your offer better. That's why I often start my USP section off with a short credibility booster;

"Hi, my name's Nathan Fraser. I'm a copywriter and I co-host the Copywriters Podcast with David Garfinkel."

"Hi, I'm Bill Wallace. I'm a residential plumber with over 30 years of experience in the Toronto area."

"Hello there. My name is Debbi Shultz and I'm a stay-at-home mom just like you. For the last five years I haven't had to scold or punish my children a single time."

This doesn't have to be a full-on bio. It can be as short as one sentence. It just needs to give them a feel for who you are and why they should care about what you have to say. Oh, and this section should be written in first-person perspective, even if the rest of your sales page isn't. It'll help draw a better connection between you and your reader.

The Overcomer USP

Another way to define your USP is by calling out a common frustration in your market and explaining why your solution is different. This is a great way to overcome objections, right off the bat, and set yourself apart as the best option. Of course, you want to be truthful. Don't go making up wild claims you can't follow through on.

Let's say you sell tennis balls to people who play fetch with their dogs. Other tennis balls are great. They're soft. You can throw them long distances. But they're green, which means they tend to get lost in the grass.

Your ball is different. It's bright orange, so it'll never get lost in the grass. Your dog can see it clearly, even when it rolls into the field. It's easy to find, even on a cloudy day. Make sure you point out that difference and explain why it matters to your readers.

"Our balls are orange, so your dog can always find them."

Okay, that one might need a little work, but you get the point. You need to spell it out for your reader. What makes you different and why should they care?

You can use either the Personal Brand USP, or the Overcomer USP, or a combination of both. Now that they know you have a solution to their problem; how can they be sure it's the right solution for them? Convince them with your USP.

SECTION 4 - FEATURES AND BENEFITS
Here's What People Are Really Buying

What do you think of when someone says the word "Features"?

If you're like most people, you probably thought about technical specs.

This chest is made of solid oak. This car has anti-lock brakes. The backyard is one square acre. We're open 24 hours. Stuff like that, right? You know, the features.

Well, every website needs a "Features" section. So, you make a list of features, put a bullet point in front of each one, and call it done. Easy-peasy.

If that's how you write your "Features" section, you're losing at least half your sales. Here's why; most people don't make their buying decisions based on logic. We like to tell ourselves we do, but it's a lie. We decide to buy something based on our emotions, then we look for logical reasons to back that emotional decision up. So, yes, you need to list out the logical reasons to buy. But you also need to include the emotional reasons to buy.

Here's how you write a powerfully persuasive "Features" section for your sales page.

First, list out all the features of your product or service. Then, go through and list how each feature translates into a benefit for your reader. Explain why each feature matters. This is what they really care about. Your job here is to make it clear what they get when they buy.

Don't assume they can make the connection between features and benefits by themselves. The more work they have to do in figuring this out, the fewer sales you'll get in return. Spell each one out for them. The better you do this, the less they have to think about it, and the more likely they are to mindlessly hit that "Buy Now" button, later on down the page.

So, if your iPod has 64 gigs of memory, tell them how many songs or audiobooks that translates into. Tell them how they'll be able to keep the party going when the DJ runs out of records. Explain how they'll be able to learn a new skill while they commute to work. If it's light as a feather, tell them how easy it is to jog with. Don't sell the technology. Sell the transformation.

If the house has a big backyard, paint them a picture of how great their neighborhood cookouts will be. If there's a spacious living room, sell movie nights with the whole family. In other words, don't sell the house, sell the home.

If you're open 24 hours, let them know it means you'll be there whenever they need you. Explain how each feature benefits them.

Sell the Sizzle, Not the Steak

Sure, you should still title this section as "Features." You can have the word "Features" bolded and enclosed with H1 tags. But don't make it only about the features.

People don't buy the features. They buy the benefits those features entail. List out each feature. Then get in and really explain how each feature will benefit your reader.

Avatar-Specific Benefits

If you want to take your sales page to the next level, drill down deep and start listing off some avatar-specific benefits.

Doing this requires knowing who exactly you're going after and why each benefit would matter to them. It takes some extra work, a little more thinking, and maybe a bit more research, but the extra sales you get in return will make it well worth your while.

So, what are avatar-specific benefits?

Well, let's say you sell luxury sports cars. You've got a nice red convertible for sale and 3 different types of people who might be interested in buying it. Depending on who your typical visitor is, the benefits to focus on will vary wildly.

Let's say you took all the features and boiled them down to one main benefit; increased self-esteem. How would that one benefit change based upon who your average website visitor might be?

1.) Teenage Boy in High School

For Tom, a senior in high school, cruising the strip with his friends might be the thing to focus on. Help him see himself winning a drag race or pulling up to his prom date's house in his shiny new car. These are the benefits that would most likely resonate with him.

2.) Female Freelance Marketing Consultant

Sarah works in a male-dominated industry. She knows her clients are always second guessing her skills. When she pulls up to a meeting in her brand-new convertible, clients know right away she's good at what she does. Her success is visible. It gives her the confidence she needs to go in and close sales like never before. That's what driving a new luxury car means to her.

3.) Mid-40's Single Dad

Jeff is re-entering the dating scene after 20 years of marriage. The girl he's picking up tonight is way out of his league. He's planned a delicious dinner at an expensive restaurant, followed by a romantic walk along the beach. He'd be shaking in his boots right now if it wasn't for the fact he's picking up his date in a brand-new convertible. That first impression will set a positive tone for the rest of their evening, and he knows it.

Each Avatar has a Different Reason for Buying

You have the same features, the same main benefit, but a bunch of different specific benefits, depending on your target avatar. The deeper you dig on figuring what a specific feature means to your exact website visitor, the more sales you'll make as a result.

SECTION 5 - MAKE YOUR OFFER / A CALL TO ACTION
Timid Salesmen Have Skinny Kids

Zig Ziglar made the above statement famous, and it's absolutely true. If you're afraid to ask for the sale, get ready for a lifetime of empty dinner plates. The same rule applies to your sales page. At some point, you have to try and make the sale.

Actually, we're gonna ask for the sale a couple times. This is just the first. If they feel like you understand their problem and you laid out benefits that matter to them, a lot of readers will be ready to buy. You need only show them the way.

There are a couple of different ways to start this section. You can go with a simple name drop of your offer. Something like; "Introducing: The Incredible Orange Tennis Ball ". You can focus on the main benefit they'll derive. Something like; "Never Lose Your Dog's Tennis Ball Again". The point is, you're making an offer. The title of the section should make that clear.

Oh, and don't worry about the awkward transition from informing them about your offer to asking them for money. I'll show you how to smoothly work your way from one to the other before your reader even knows what hit them.

The most common way to transition into your offer is with the header for your offer section. This will be the bolded font at the beginning of your offer. Something like "Introducing" and then follow that with the name of your product or service.

You can also follow with the main benefit you're selling on. An example would be something like "Introducing the Tennis Ball That Never Gets Lost in the Grass" or "Introducing a Brand-New Way to Impress Your Hardest to Please Clients". Then, hit these four points to transition into your Call to Action.

1.) **What Do They Get?**

You have to spell out exactly what they'll receive.

Will it be a physical product or a digital product? Will it be an online course or a live, one-on-one training? Is the yoga mat made of high-grade rubber or a bio-friendly, hemp-based plastic?

Whatever they get, spell it out in detail. List every aspect for them. This way, you're not asking them to walk into a dark room.

2.) **How Is It Delivered?**

Will it come in the mail? Can they pick it up at the store? Will it come through email, or through a member's only area on your website? Is there more than one shipping option available? Will it arrive instantly, within 2 days, or by the end of the work week?

Let them know exactly what they can expect to happen after they hit the "Buy Now" button.

3.) **What Transformation Will They Get?**

This is what they're really buying, so paint a vivid picture for them.

Will they get six-pack abs and look sexier? Will they get peace of mind, knowing their children are safe and protected? Will they get the envy of all those who doubted them?

This "new way of being" should be explicit in the offer. There should be no doubt as to what their life will look like after they decide to buy. This should also be the last thing you focus on before calling them to action.

4.) **What Should They Do to Get It? Your Call to Action**

Now that you've got them imagining what they'll get, tell them what they need to do in order to get it. Spell it out for them. Don't count on them to figure it out for themselves.

Give them a clear and definitive CTA (Call to Action).

"Pick up the phone and order now."

"Visit our website to get yours today."

"Click the link below."

"Fill out this form and send it to..."

Make sure the copy is specific and leaves no room for confusion. After all, a confused mind decides nothing. The more work you do here to make it clear for them, the more sales you'll make.

Lastly - and this is a mistake I see way too many copywriters make - don't let your copy "sell from the heel". You've been going strong through your whole sales page. Don't let up now. Words like "might", "intended to", "could help with" all signify a lack of confidence in your offer. If you show a lack of confidence, they'll lose confidence. Don't let that happen.

I call these kinds of words and phrases "weasel words". Avoid them at all cost. You'll kill your conversion rates if your CTA closes out soft and starts selling from the heel.

Follow these four steps, in this order, and close out strong. This will get you the most sales possible from your sales page.

SECTION 6 - BULLETS

How to Stop Skimmers Dead in Their Tracks

People are busy, lazy, and easily distracted. This is doubly true for people on the internet. A lot of people hit a big sales page and immediately go into skim-reading mode.

Bullets are great for these kinds of readers. They stop them in their tracks and pull them back into your sales copy. Bullets are bite-sized chunks of information that break up your sales page and make it easier to read.

They also present a great opportunity to restate your most persuasive selling points. This may seem a bit redundant, but like I said, not everybody will read your entire sales page. If you want to make absolutely sure your reader catches something, placing it in a bullet is a good way to do it.

Now, a lot of people can't write a good bullet to save their life. They think a bullet should just make a point about the thing they're selling. Nothing could be further from the truth.

So, what should you do instead?

Above all else, bullets should evoke curiosity in your reader. You want to tease your reader, hint at what they'll get, and leave them desperate to find out more.

People can't stand an open loop. They want to have all the loose ends neatly tied up for them. Your "Bullets" section should fray up some of those ends in a way that compels them to buy your service or product and get closure on the things you hinted at.

What follows are 10 different bullet types, why they work, and how to write them. You'll also get a few examples of each one. Let's begin.

10 Different Types of Bullets

Here's a list of my 10 favorite bullet types. Many of them can be used in combination with each other. I'll give some examples of this as we go. Also, keep in mind that it's good to vary up your bullets. Using the same bullet type over and over again will get boring for your reader and you can't bore people into buying.

When transitioning into your "Bullets" section, use one of the following phrases, followed by a colon, like so:

Order now and you'll get:

Discover:

Your vacation includes:

Get the point?

Okay, here we go.

The Blind Bullet

"Blind" bullets are also known as "Teaser" bullets. They tease out a benefit the reader will get, without giving away any specific details. They can also promise to reveal some sort of secret knowledge to the reader once they've purchased what you're selling.

These kinds of bullets should be juicy enough to get them excited, but vague enough to keep them curious.

Examples:

- The most common deductible you could use to save over 38% on your tax bill that almost nobody knows about
- A simple way to get your teeth white as snow without having to visit the dentist
- The real reason your husband started going to the gym again after years of not caring about his bulging

- belly
- The home remedy your doctor uses when no one's looking

See how these bullets tease out some secret knowledge, while concealing path to get there? That's what "Blind" bullets are all about. Reveal the destination as a way to sell the map.

The Contrarian Bullet

Sometimes you want to shake your readers up to get their attention. Nothing does that better than a good old-fashioned "Contrarian" bullet. This kind of bullet is for people who like making hamburgers out of sacred cows.

"Contrarian" bullets expose why a commonly-held belief is ass-backwards. You're calling out a practice that nobody else dares question. Your reader may know deep-down that what you're saying is true, but only you had the balls to say it. These bullets help position you as an alternative to the mainstream, planting your flag on a hill for others to rally behind.

Note; Only use this type of bullet if you have a very convincing reason as to why the popular belief on something is wrong.

Examples:

- Why milk DOESN'T actually do a body good
- 4 reasons NOT to waste time building a website for your business
- Doing all those sit-ups might be the reason you can't lose your belly fat. We'll show you why.

Each of these takes a commonly held belief and turns it on its head. If you have a good reason to go against the grain, put it in a "Contrarian" bullet to get the most mileage out of it.

The Benefit Bullet

"Benefit" bullets are also known as "Open" bullets. They're almost the opposite of "Blind" bullets. With these, you want to spell out the benefit in as much detail as possible.

There's no need to be mysterious or vague. Tell them exactly what they get and how they benefit from it. These are often the easiest bullets to write if you know what your reader is really looking for.

Examples:

- Get rock-hard abs in just 5 minutes a day
- Sell your house by the end of next week
- Never have a bad hair day again

"Benefit" bullets should be short and to the point. They should lay out exactly what the reader gets, as an end result of going with your offer.

The If/Then Bullet

Sometimes the offer looks great, but your reader needs to know it'll work for them. "If/Then" bullets help your readers qualify themselves. They work great for people who are on the fence about your offer.

The basic layout of an "If/Then" bullet goes like this:

If you can do this, you can get that. But the subconscious message is; "If this is true about you, then this is something you should buy."

Examples:

- If you can spare 5 minutes a day, you can earn up to $23,000 in a single month

- If you're over the age of 35 and a non-smoker, United Health can help you get low-cost health insurance today
- If you've ever dreamed of building a better life for yourself, this is the chance you've been waiting for

Use these bullets to overcome objections your reader might have about your offer. If you know why they're still on the fence about buying, then this kind of bullet can help push them over.

The Numbered Bullet

"Numbered" bullets are great because they add a sense of tangibility to your offer. If people can see multiple uses or benefits, it increases the perceived value. Now they're getting three things for the price of one.

Note; Numbers in bullets should never be typed out.

Use "3" rather than "three" and so on. Using the actual number is more attention grabbing and also gives the bullet a weighted sense of "value".

"Numbered" bullets also work great in combination with other styled bullets, as seen earlier in the "Contrarian" bullets section.

Examples:

- 4 simple ways to cut down on your sugar consumption
- 5 mind-blowing techniques for a more productive morning
- 3 of the best speakers in the industry

"Numbered" bullets are great for stopping skimmers dead in their tracks and pulling them back into your sales page. Make sure to include at least one "Numbered" bullet in every bullets section of your sales copy.

The "What To" Bullet

Often times, people are looking for direction and clarity on how to solve their problem. This is where "What To" bullets shine. They offer your reader a feeling of hope that you can provide the answer they're looking for. They tease at the prospect of a better future. They also help establish you as a trusted authority in their minds.

Examples:

- What to do if she starts losing interest in your relationship
- What to tell a client when they ask about your prices
- What to wear on your first date when you know she's out of your league

This kind of bullet can be combined with "Numbered" bullets, "Blind" bullets, "If/Then" bullets, and others.

Examples:

- 3 things to bring on your camping trip to make it unforgettable
- What to do when the tax man comes knocking
- If you're running late on your way to the airport, do this and you'll be able to skip past all the people waiting in line at the TSA

The "What Never" Bullet

Just like "What To" bullets, "What Never" bullets offer a clear sense of direction and understanding, but in the opposite way. They're great for people who are skeptical or prone to look out for danger. Since this is part of our basic survival instincts, these bullets work well for almost every audience. They work especially well for the finance, survival, and weight loss industries.

Like other bullets on this list, you can use them in combination for packing an even bigger punch.

Examples:

- What you should never tell your significant other on your honeymoon
- 3 foods to never eat on an airplane
- What never to pack on a cross-country vacation

"What Never" bullets work great for info-products, newsletters and the like. They also make the reader feel like you're looking out for their best interest. Use this to your advantage.

The "How To" Bullet

Another great bullet type for info-products is the "How To" bullet. These work great for promising a transformation in the ability of your reader. Use them to show the things they'll be able to do or understand after buying your product or service.

I like to transition into "How To" bullets with a phrase like "You'll discover:" or "Exclusive training reveals:"

Examples:

- How to get free money for college
- How to turn a boring salad into a satisfying daytime meal
- 5 ways to shed 15 pounds in the next 30 days

These are all variations on the "How To" bullet. Play around with them and see what works best for you.

The "Reason Why" Bullet

If your reader is looking for a solution, but also for answers - "Reason Why" bullets will get their attention. They promise to enlighten your reader and show them a better way.

These kinds of bullets work great for info-products, online courses, books, and newsletters. If your reader is looking for enlightenment or to avoid being made the fool, "Reason Why" bullets will do the trick.

Examples:

- The reason why your girlfriend won't video chat after 9 p.m.
- The reason why your doctor won't tell you about healthy alternatives to harmful chemicals
- The real reason you can't make a million dollars in your current career (and what you can do to change it)

Some people are all-too-happy to remain willfully ignorant. Others pride themselves on having the secret knowledge that most people lack. If your reader is the latter, sprinkle some "Reasons Why" throughout your list of bullets. They'll work like a charm.

The Problem/Solution Bullet

I've heard these bullets referred to as "Reverse Hook" bullets. I call them "Problem/Solution" bullets because that's how they're laid out. They point out an obvious problem in your market and explain how your offer solves that problem.

These bullets often combine elements of the "Contrarian"

bullet with elements of "Blind" bullets or "Benefit" bullets. If that seems confusing, check out the examples below and it'll make perfect sense for you.

Examples:

- Do you suffer from motion sickness? Eat this common snack before your next road trip and never feel nauseous while traveling again.

- Most workout programs ignore the fact that diet plays a huge role in getting you the results you desire. Nutri-Fit comes with a diet plan tailored both for your workout regimen and your body type.

- 37% percent of Facebook Ad campaigns never convert a single prospect. Use this simple targeting strategy and you'll be on-boarding new clients by the end of this week.

These kinds of bullets speak directly to what your prospect is already thinking. They meet them where they're at, and point them in the right direction. Because they start off in agreement, your reader finds the second half to be much more believable.

People don't trust advertising. By addressing their doubts head-on, you help alleviate them. You can use "Problem/Solution" bullets to win over the most skeptical of readers.

Note: this is not an all-encompassing list of every bullet type out there.

As you continue to study copywriting, you'll likely stumble across tons of other kinds of bullets. Like I mentioned before, you can come up with new bullet types by simply combining the above examples.

This is just a list of the most common and easiest to use bullet types out there. Have fun and get creative. Once you get good at writing bullets, you'll find you can use them for laying out your entire sales page and even for coming up with that perfect headline.

SECTION 7 - TESTIMONIALS
How to Gain Instant Trust and Credibility

Most people don't like being a guinea pig. Especially when it comes to the spending of their hard-earned money. Before we take a leap of faith, we like to look around and see if others have safely gone where we're about to go.

On a sales page, we add this kind of "social proof" by using testimonials. This way, your visitor gets to see other people singing your praises, rather than just you boasting about your offer. If they see your product or service worked for others, they're a lot more likely to believe it'll work for them as well.

You can have a page on your site that's dedicated exclusively to showcasing your testimonials, but you want to have two or three testimonials on your sales page as well. This will go a long way in making people comfortable with pulling out their credit cards and doing business with you.

Keep this in mind, readers view testimonials as an average. So, if one testimonial sucks, it pulls down the persuasion power of the other two it sits beside. Only include the most compelling parts of your most compelling testimonials on your sales page. You can include a "Read More" link to your full Testimonials Page if you feel the need to do so. But only the best of the best should be showcased on your sales page.

Also, people tend to give more importance to things at the beginning and end of a list, while forgetting whatever landed in the middle. For this reason, I plot out my testimonials in the order of 2, 3, 1.

The second most impressive testimonial comes first, followed by the least impressive of the three. The last one they read will have the most sticking power, so I always reserve that spot for my most powerful testimonial. This is due to something called "Recency Bias".

Think of it like a reverse-sandwich.

In a sandwich, you have bread, then the good stuff, followed by more bread. When laying out your testimonials, do the opposite. Give them the good stuff, then the less-good stuff, and finish it off with the best stuff.

Great testimonial.

Good testimonial.

Best testimonial.

In that order.

What to Include in Your Testimonials Section

First off, make sure they look real. Include the full names, professions, and pictures of the people you have featured. If possible, include contact information for everyone who provided a testimonial. This last one isn't absolutely necessary, but it never hurts have it listed. If your testimonials look fake or contrived, it makes everything else on your sales page look less convincing.

There are three basic types of testimonials. In this next section, we'll take a look at each one and how they work.

Experience-Based Testimonials

These testimonials help the reader know what they will experience if they buy from you. They need to be from someone your prospective reader can relate with. The goal is to paint a picture of what it's like to enjoy what you offer.

"Tom and his crew were clean, respectful, and a joy to work with."

"The wedding cake Jane made for us was beautiful and

delicious. The whole party agreed."

"Camp Evergreen is a great retreat. The lake was perfect and the hiking was amazing. My family and I had a great time."

These are all examples of "Experience-Based" testimonials. If your reader is looking for a particular type of experience, these types of testimonials will do the trick.

Results-Based Testimonials

Some people are more interested in results than an experience. They don't care what the process looks like. They care about what the process delivers. For these people, "Results-Based" testimonials work best.

Like the above type of testimonials, these ones need to be from someone your reader can relate with. They want to know it will work for them. The best way to show that is by proving it worked for someone just like them.

"With Nutri-Slim, I was able to lose 15 pounds in five days; and the weight stayed off."

"After hiring Nathan to write our sales page, we saw an instant increase of 3% on our conversions."

"Tax-Pro Small Business found $62,327 in deductions that our in-house accountant missed. The software paid for itself many times over in the first year of using it."

If your reader is looking for results, these are the type of testimonials to focus on for your sales page.

Colleague-Based Testimonials

This is where you have an esteemed colleague in your field recommend you. These work best if the person giving the testimonial has some celebrity in your niche. Your reader might not trust you yet, but if someone they trust is vouching for you, it'll help them rest easier about buying from you.

These types of testimonials give off the "Halo Effect". You become more trustworthy by being associated with people they already see as trusted authorities. To illustrate my point, here's a testimonial I received from one of the greatest copywriters in the world:

"I'm on a first-name, speed-dial basis with many of the top marketers in the entrepreneurial space. But when it came to marketing my own message, I've never found anyone who even comes close to Nathan Fraser."
- David Garfinkel
Owner, Garfinkel Coaching

These types of testimonials can also get the person reading your sales page to believe that, by buying what you offer, they'll be able to be more like the person giving the testimonial. Think: Michael Jordan selling Nike shoes or John Lee Dumas promoting Click-Funnels. "If I buy these shoes, I'll be able to dunk like Mike." "If I buy Click Funnels, I'll be as successful as JLD."

You get the point.

Testimonials work. Use them in your sales page.

How to Get Amazing Testimonials

Customers are notorious for writing bad testimonials. It might be a glowing review, but it'll be a horrible testimonial. After all, they're not copywriters. They don't know what a good testimonial should look like. Their testimonials end up being long-winded and not very convincing.

Most business owners leave the quality of their testimonials up to chance. Here's what to do instead. Ask for testimonials right away; right after they've made their purchase or right after they've gotten their results.

Buyers are the happiest right after they've bought what you sell. They're also looking for ways to reinforce their buying decision. Make sure to h it them up right after you've delivered the product, service, or result. While they're in this "honeymoon stage" is when you'll get the most positive feedback from them.

Also, help them along with what kind of feedback you need from them. I'm looking for the answers to five questions in particular. To ensure I get the answers I need, I'll often have my questions pre-written on a feedback form with an area for them to give their reply.

Here are variations of the five questions I always ask:

1.) Please describe the problem you were dealing with that led to buy from us.

2.) How was that problem affecting you?

3.) How did we solve that problem for you?

4.) What was the best thing about your experience with our solution?

5.) How do you feel, now that the problem is solved?

Then I take their answers and turn those answers into their testimonial. Sometimes it takes a little re-wording or editing to get the flow I'm looking for. Once I've got something I like, I send them back what they wrote, show them my edit, and ask them if my edit stays true to what they were trying to say. If so, I'll get their permission to use my edit as their testimonial on my sales page.

Note: Always get permission before using someone's testimonial. If you can get it in writing or through email, even better. Also, check the legalities of your industry, as far as what kinds of testimonials are allowed. Not all industries can use every kind of testimonial.

SECTION 8 - FREQUENTLY ASKED QUESTIONS

The Most Under-Utilized Section of Your Sales Page

Today's consumers want to know they're making an informed buying decision. That's why salespeople are paid so well. Salespeople sit there and answer all the questions. They make the buyer feel like an informed consumer. Answering questions is an important part of the sales process. If you can't have a salesperson on hand, having a "Frequently Asked Questions" section on your sales page is the next best thing.

Yes, you can get chat-based customer service plug-ins for your website. You can even program chatbots to save time or money on hiring an actual assistant. But you'll still find yourself answering the same questions, over and over again. So, having a section to address those questions is a no-brainer.

Aside from that, your FAQ section has the opportunity to do some major selling. You can use it to filter out any "bad fit" customers or clients. You can also use it to overcome a lot of objections your reader might be having.

I'll often include questions I know will segment out the people my offer isn't right for. When doing so, I try to "make the skeleton dance" a little. "Making the skeleton dance" is when you take something they see as a bad thing and show how it's actually a good thing, for the right people.

If my price is higher than they expected, I'll explain how I only work with one client at a time to give them my full attention and energy. Or, I'll explain how we only use the most advanced technology and we're only for the people who take their craft very seriously. Not only will this help you avoid chargebacks and refund requests by "filtering out" the wrong people, it also helps the right people feel more secure in buying from you. Most importantly, you can use your FAQ section to overcome any unwarranted objections your reader might still have.

Overcoming Objections in Your FAQ's

My favorite area of the sales page to overcome objections with is the FAQ section. Most of the questions I list will be there to overcome their objections to buying. I'll mix in some "filtering out" questions so it doesn't start to feel "salesy". But convincing them to buy is still my main goal with this section.

First, ask yourself what objections your reader might have? If you've previously sold your offer in person, what objections came up most often in your sales conversations? This is just a starting point. You can, and should, dig a little deeper. Seek out the most common objections people have to your particular offer.

Write these questions out in a way your reader would likely ask them. Then, answer the questions in a clear and honest manner. If your solution helps them avoid what they're afraid of, show them why they have nothing to worry about. If you can't overcome their objection honestly, use this as a "filtering out" question.

Questions to ask and overcome include:

- How have they been burned by similar offers in the past?
- If so, how is your offer different?
- What might make them think this won't work for them?
- Will they object to your price?
- If so, how can you justify it?

- Will they trust you?
- If not, can you give them good reason to?

Depending on your unique situation, there will be a number of different objections to overcome. Don't ignore them. Even if you don't bring them up on your sales page, your reader will still have them nagging around in the back of their mind. It's always better to address them and move on.

Are they worried about durability? Explain how you only use the sturdiest of materials.

Have they tried something similar that didn't work for them? Show how your version is different in a way that addresses their concern and sets them at ease. Handle each objection with a benefit-driven claim to the opposite, give proof, then re-state the benefit for them.

Here's an example:

Q: I've never heard of you before. How can I trust your marketing agency is right for me?

A: We've worked behind the scenes with some of your favorite entrepreneurs. Our team was responsible for (viral marketing example A) and we work closely with (recognizable client B) and (recognizable client C). If you haven't heard of us, it's because we spend our time promoting our clients, not ourselves.

See how that works?

People are more skeptical now than ever before. You have to meet that skepticism with reasons to believe in what you're selling.

You can always provide case studies, testimonials, and demonstrations on your sales page. These work great for taking on skepticism. The FAQ section isn't the only place to overcome objections, but it's one of the best.

SECTION 9 - YOUR SECOND CALL TO ACTION

Another Chance to Buy

By now, many of your readers will be ready to buy. Don't make them wait any longer.

After the FAQ section is a great place to include a second Call to Action. The reason why is that you've just eliminated any objections they might have been holding on to. You don't have to repeat everything you had in your original CTA, but give them another chance to click "Buy Now".

I like to make my second Call to Action a condensed version of the first. Quickly restate what they get, including the main benefit or transformation. Then, duplicate your original "Buy Now" button.

This section doesn't have to be much more than that. Give them another chance to buy, then move on to your final bits of persuasion.

SECTION 10 - ADDING SCARCITY

How to Get Sales Today and End Procrastination Forever

Here's one of the biggest mistakes in life I ever made.

I was living with a girl I used to date. We'd stayed friends after a number of years and decided to move back in together. It was a mutually beneficial arrangement.

I still loved her, and I'm pretty sure she still loved me, but I never told her how I felt. Partially out of fear, but mostly out of selfishness. I had everything I wanted from her, and I didn't have to give up my freedom to keep it.

This went on for a couple of years. I kept dragging her along without giving her the commitment she deserved. Then, she started talking to someone else.

I saw my window of opportunity closing and knew I had to act quickly.

One day, while driving her around, I worked up the nerve to tell her how I felt. I knew I was about to lose her, so I laid it all on the line. But it was too little, too late. She rejected me and my heart was broken.

If only I'd acted sooner.

You see, as people, we're more likely to take action once we realize our inaction will lead to a lost opportunity. For that reason, adding an element of scarcity can drive people to take action right away. If you don't give them a reason to act now, they'll put it off until tomorrow. But tomorrow, like your sales, might never come.

Examples of Scarcity

There are three main ways to work scarcity into your offer. These all work as a kind of "take away" offer. If your reader is still on the fence about committing, this can be enough to push them over.

One thing to keep in mind though; the scarcity must be real and reasonable. "Only 5 copies of this digital eBook left" won't work. If you try to trick people with a false sense of scarcity, they'll see right through it and feel insulted. This will lose you sales.

You don't always have to include an element of scarcity on your sales page. But if you decide to, use the one that makes the most sense for your offer.

Limited Time Offer

These work great for holiday or event-based sales.

"This weekend only."

"From now until Christmas."

"While the boss is away on vacation."

You can also run a Limited Time Offer for Grand Openings or for beta users of a new software, product or program. This is probably the easiest form of scarcity to pull off if you have a legitimate reason for the limitations.

Limited Supply Offer

These work great for limited prints, warehouse liquidations, and slot-based offers.

"I only have 5 slots available at this price."

"Limited to 100 signed and certified editions."

"We've only got 3 left in stock."

Again, this probably won't work for an eBook or an online course. But it's perfect for a physical product or a service that doesn't scale very well. If you're going to use it, make sure it makes sense for the offer.

Exclusivity Offer

This is the hardest one to pull off but it can end up being the most profitable. You're basically saying your offer is only for certain people. This makes the unqualified people want it more. It also makes the qualified people feel like they're part of an elite group when they take you up on your offer.

"I only work with people making over 7 figures."

"We only admit the best and the brightest."

"Must go to a caring home."

By explicitly stating who you aren't for, it makes your offer instantly more appealing. This can also result in a justification for higher prices. While the Limited Time and Limited Supply offers tend to indicate a price decrease, Exclusivity Offers tend to mean a price increase.

Like I said, Exclusivity Offers are the hardest to pull off, but they're often the most profitable way to add scarcity to your sales page.

SECTION 11 - RISK REVERSAL

Put Your Money Where Your Mouth Is

"Can I trust that I'll be happy with what you sell me?"

Like it or not, that's the main question going through someone's mind when they reach the end of your sales page.

If they buy something from Walmart and they don't like it, they can take it back and get a refund. If they hire a local company to come out and paint their home, they can call up the painter if there's an issue with the color. But what can they do if they're not happy with something they bought online? How can they trust they'll be taken care of if something goes wrong?

You have to set them at ease, and you do that with your "Risk Reversal" section.

A "Risk Reversal" is something that takes the risk off of their shoulders and places it solely on yours. This way, they know you stand behind what you sell. You can do this in a few different ways.

Money Back Guarantee

The easiest way is to offer a Money Back Guarantee. Yes, some people might ask for a refund. But, for every refund request your guarantee invites, you'll get a bunch of sales you wouldn't have otherwise gotten.

Most of us wouldn't feel right about keeping money from an unsatisfied customer. If someone wanted to return our product, we'd happily refund their money. So, why not make that a part of our marketing? Why not spell it out in your guarantee?

Just make sure your refund policy is clear and prevents you

from being taken advantage of. If they buy the supplement, take it as directed, and don't see the expected result, make them send the empty bottle back for a full refund. But only if they can prove they took it as directed and followed your refund policy to a T.

Free Trial Offer

Another way to set your visitors at ease is by offering a Free Trial Offer. This way, they can try before they buy. This works great for SaaS products and other digital services. A lot of businesses have a "Freemium" offer that grants free access to a limited version of the full offer. "Try before you buy" is a great way to eliminate risk on the buyers end. Just make sure you state it clearly if they'll be charged after the trial period is over. Otherwise you'll see a lot of chargebacks, which may result in getting your payment processor or merchant account shut down.

Trust Signaling

One last way to put your buyers at ease is to showcase accreditations you might have from any consumer advocacy groups. If you're in good standing with the Better Business Bureau, local Chamber of Commerce or you've been featured in Consumers Digest, include their logos on your website. This lets your visitors know you can be trusted. If you've won any awards or recognitions in your industry, make sure to include them here.

Even a simple PayPal logo can instill an extra layer of trust in doing business with you. When someone goes to fill out your purchase form, having a trusted payment processor logo will put them at ease. Seeing logos from the BBB or an award your company recently won will compound that effect.

SECTION 12 - POSTSCRIPT SELLING
"Act Now, and We'll Include…"

When I was a kid, my parents used to watch reruns of an old show called Columbo. It was about a detective who always got his man.

Throughout the show, he'd interview a bunch of different suspects as he zeroed in on the guilty party. Very often, it would look like the killer got away with it, until Colombo uttered his infamous line… "Oh, one more thing."

Then, he'd drop the final question on them; the one that dismantled their whole alibi. They were so close to walking away, but he snatched them up at the last minute. That's how I like to think of my "P.S." section. If I haven't got them yet, what's the one last thing I can do to persuade them?

There are a couple different ways to go about doing this. One is to do what I call "The Value Stack". Simply restate everything they get with your offer. Attach a dollar amount to each individual aspect of what you're giving them. Then, tally up the total and compare it to the lower price of your offer.

"If you were to buy all of these items separately, you'd pay well over X. But, if you buy now, you'll get everything shown here for the low-low price of (less than X)."

Another thing you can do here is to inform them of any bonus items they get with your offer. Bonus items should complement what they're already getting and make buying a no-brainer. If they're buying website hosting, throw in a free course on how to install WordPress and get great SEO. If they're buying a set of kitchen knives, throw in a solid oak knife holder and cutting board set.

Again, make sure the bonus items are a good fit for what you're selling. It's also a good idea to put a price tag on the actual value of their bonuses. That way it doesn't look like you're just trying to offload your worthless, excess inventory on them.

"That's a combined value of $927, and you get it all for free if you order within the next 30 minutes."

This type of last-minute selling worked great on the old school infomercials. Now, thanks to browser cookies and countdown timers, you can make them work on your sales page as well. With or without a countdown timer, having a "P.S." section can be the final nudge your reader needs to turn them into a buyer.

SECTION 12.5 – LAST CALL
Going for the Glory

This is your final Call to Action (CTA), your last chance to make the sale; Finish out strong.

Remember, don't use any weasel words. Don't sell from the heel. Let them know you're confident in what you sell so they can feel confident in buying it.

You can copy and paste your CTA from earlier, or you can write a new one for each Call to Action. Many sales pages just copy and paste, but it's really up to whatever you prefer.

The places I mentioned in this guide aren't the only places you can call people to action. I've written some very long form sales pages where I put a new call to action after every section. I like to give visitors as many chances to buy as possible.

As long as it feels right, you can pretty much put a "Call to Action" anywhere on your sales page. The places I listed in this template are just what I've found to be universally applicable.

Play around with it. See what feels right. If you want to get fancy, add a heat map to your website and make sure you have your CTA's in areas where visitors spend a lot of time.

My only rule is this; make sure you have more than one "Call to Action". When people are ready to buy, don't make them search through your sales page for the order form. Have it right there, waiting for them.

FIN

Okay, now you're ready to write your own sales page.

I've just given you my favorite formula to use when I'm writing sales pages for myself and my clients. It hits all the bases and has a very natural flow to its structure. Between my own products and those of my clients, I can trace back at least a quarter million dollars in sales to this template over the last few years.

It's easy to follow and easy to flesh out. I can't guarantee you'll see the same results. But I can guarantee it's a template that works.

Whether you write copy for clients or for your own website, this template will make it a whole lot easier. And chances are, you'll see an increase in conversions because of it.

In Closing

I hope you've found this guide useful. It's the resource I wish I had when I first started selling things online. I've been writing my own sales copy for over five years now and writing for clients almost as long. Time and time again, this is the template I fall back on. It just works.

I've been blessed to work with David Garfinkel on the Copywriters Podcast, and I'd be lying if I said his influence didn't weigh heavily on this book. He's been an invaluable mentor to me and I can't tell you how grateful I am to work with him.

As in-depth as this guide may be, it's not meant to be an end-all guide to copywriting. I didn't even get into how I edit my sales copy, how I test my sales pages, and a number of other subtle things that can make a huge difference in sales.

This template is more of a jumping-off point; a way to get

you off to a great start. If you'd like further help, I'd love to make myself available. For consulting and copy critiques, you can find me at my official website.

    https://copyandfunnels.com/

ABOUT THE AUTHOR

Nathan Fraser is a podcast producer and copywriter, living in Colorado.

He spends most of his time writing sales letters and recording podcasts for his clients. When he's not doing that, you can find him stirring up trouble on social media or spending time with the people he loves.

He also writes bios for himself in the third person.

If you enjoyed this book, you can find more of his work over at https://copyandfunnels.com/

Printed in Great Britain
by Amazon

43176915R00040